INDIA AND THE TARIFF PROBLEM

INDIA AND THE TARIFF PROBLEM

H. B. LEES-SMITH M.A.

GYAN

Published by

Gyan Publishing House
5, Ansari Road
Daryaganj, New Delhi-110002
Phone: 011-47034999, 9811692060
E-mail: books@gyanbooks.com

Distribution Network
gyanbooks.com
India, USA, Canada, UK, Australia, France

ISBN: 978-81-212-8838-5 (PB)
First Published, 1909

2nd Impression 2023

Printed at: Gyan Press, Delhi.

INDIA AND THE TARIFF PROBLEM
Author: H. B. Lees-Smith

INDIA AND THE TARIFF PROBLEM

BY

H. B. LEES SMITH.

INDIA AND THE TARIFF PROBLEM

BY

H. B. LEES-SMITH M.A.

PROFESSOR OF PUBLIC ADMINISTRATION IN THE UNIVERSITY OF BRISTOL; LECTURER TO THE LONDON SCHOOL OF ECONOMICS AND POLITICAL SCIENCE; ASSISTANT EDITOR OF THE "ECONOMIC JOURNAL"; CHAIRMAN OF EXECUTIVE COMMITTEE OF RUSKIN COLLEGE, OXFORD

LONDON
CONSTABLE & COMPANY LTD
1909

PREFACE

This essay is based upon a series of lectures delivered for the Government of Bombay. Some of the subjects with which it deals are discussed more fully in "Studies in Indian Economics," which will be issued by the Government of Bombay at the same time as this little book.

The last two chapters discuss the recent proposals for preferential tariffs with India. There is one question which can be treated more appropriately here than in the body of the essay. I have been asked by a number of the leaders of educated opinion in India to state clearly what I consider their attitude should be towards the proposals for preferential tariffs. I was informed that the reason that the Indian National Congress had pronounced no opinion on the subject was, not that they failed to realise its importance, but that they were waiting for more light. My opinion on this point can be easily deduced from the last two chapters of this essay. By preferential tariffs Great Britain will lose heavily in her Indian market. India, however, has little either to lose or gain from preferences by themselves. Nevertheless, the proposals for preferences are of the highest importance to her. If they are ever adopted by the United Kingdom, they will undoubtedly be accompanied by a return to protection. India will then have a unique opportunity of gaining her fiscal freedom. Although I have not disguised my suspicions of the prevailing protectionist sentiment of India, I wish to see her freely adopting the fiscal policy which she considers most for the good of her own people. India, of course, means for this purpose the Indian Government, acting, I sincerely hope, in conjunction with the educated opinion of the country. My advice to the leaders of Indian opinion is simple. They should make it plain that if a preferential scheme is adopted, they are willing that India should have a place in it. One fact, however, must stand out clearly. Should Great Britain adopt protection she must honourably face the consequences of her conversion, and allow to India the right to follow in her footsteps, if Indian administrators and thinkers consider it to be for the country's good.

Professor Edwin Cannan has kindly read through the manuscript of this essay, and has saved me from more than one mistake.

H. B. LEES SMITH.

BOMBAY,
February, 1909.

CONTENTS

INDIA AND THE TARIFF PROBLEM

CHAPTER I

DIVERSITY OF INDUSTRY

A DISCUSSION of the position of India under protection and preferences must be based upon her special conditions. Since many British readers are not familiar with these conditions, the first three chapters of this book will be devoted to the "descriptive economics" of India.

From two-thirds to three-fourths of the population of India are engaged in agriculture. Of the remainder a large number are weavers, carpenters, blacksmiths, and other village artisans who are as dependent upon the chances and fluctuations of agriculture as are the tillers of the soil. It is difficult for a British observer to grasp the full significance of the fact that the majority of Indians are scattered over nearly three-quarters of a million villages, each with less than five thousand inhabitants. One result, however, he can readily understand. No sooner are Western ideas introduced into such a land than there sets in an overwhelming tide of opinion against the continued ruralisation of the people. The United States, Germany, and our self-governing colonies have all refused to remain in a position in which they were producers of food and raw material—"hewers of wood and drawers of water"—for the nations with a more advanced industrial development. It is not surprising, therefore, that the cry that manufactures must be built up should be as loud in India as in these other countries. It indeed expresses one of the few opinions on which all thinkers in India, whether they are "moderates" or "extremists" or Government officials, are unanimous. To the highest type of Indian thinker the economic reason does not come first. His eyes are fixed upon the distant day when his countrymen, no longer a subject race, will be in their country what an Englishman or a Canadian is in his. There is no hope of achieving this high purpose until Indians have infused Western ideas into their national life. They must not, however, adopt them blindly, but must so mould them to their own characteristics as to transform them into truly Indian ideas. Such a task cannot be carried out by an almost entirely rural population. Agricultural peoples have many virtues, but readiness to grasp new ideas is not usually one of them. Where the rural type of mind predominates there is danger of stagnation. If, therefore, the pioneers in the new paths which are being disclosed by Western influences are to be drawn from India's own sons, she needs the quick intelligence and the progressive spirit developed by manufacturing industries of the modern type.

This was the lesson taught to the present generations of Indians by the foremost economic thinker that India has yet produced—Justice Ranade. "This dependency," he says, "has come to be regarded as a 'plantation' growing raw produce to be shipped by British agents in British ships, to be worked into fabrics by British skill and capital, and to be re-exported to the dependency by British merchants to their corresponding British firms in India and elsewhere. Except in the large Presidency towns, the country is fed, clothed, warmed, washed, lighted, helped and comforted generally by a thousand arts and industries, in the manipulation of which its sons have every day a decreasing share. The political domination of one nation by another attracts far more attention than the more formidable, though unfelt, domination which the capital enterprise and skill of one country exercise over the trade and manufactures of others. This latter domination has an insidious influence which paralyses the springs of all the varied activities which together make up the life of a nation. The progress of ruralisation in India means its rustication, *i.e.*, a loss of power and intelligence and self-dependence. Foreign competition is transferring the monopoly, not only of wealth, but what is more important, of skill, talent, and activity, to others."[1]

Arguments of this kind apply with equal force to other nations. But one feature of the position is peculiar to India. The fear of drought is the curse which Nature has laid upon the land. India lives by the

[1] "Essays in Indian Economics," by Mahadev Govind Ranade (Nateson & Co., Madras). Ranade deserves to be better known in England. He was far more than an economic thinker. Many of those who are urging on those reforms in Indian social life, such as the loosening of caste restrictions, which will profoundly modify the present Hindu system, were inspired by him. The leading spirit of the modern nationalist movement looks back to his memory with emotion. The mention of his name before an audience of educated Hindus, especially in Western India, will produce a thrill deeper than that which would answer to any other name of the last generation.

monsoons. If the rains fail during July, August, and September, the tillers of the soil are face to face with disease, starvation and death. This terrible reason for building up manufactures is one which presses more heavily upon India than upon the other nations whose example she wishes to follow. The amount of weight, however, which is to be attached to it will be better understood if we first make a survey of the present position of famine relief.

The outstanding fact in the problem of famine is that it is no longer insoluble. It has been transformed into a problem of acute unemployment. Drought will never be prevented, but we may look forward to the time when deaths from famine in India will be as unnecessary as deaths from unemployment in Great Britain. This transformation has been effected within the last fifty years. Before that period a severe drought meant inevitable death. There was no food, and all the wealth of the world could not procure it. Owing to the "immobility of foodstuffs" when crops failed in one district, death from starvation was certain, although harvests might be abundant one hundred miles away. Charity was of little use, for sufficient food was not to be procured. The position now is altogether different. Food is dear, but food is to be had. The difficulty is not lack of food, but, owing to the fact that all are thrown out of their usual employment, lack of money. Hence the problem is soluble, for the people can be given money where previously no human power could give them food.

The secret of the change is to be found partly in irrigation, but chiefly in the development of the railways. In India, as in the rest of the world, they are vitally altering not only the economic but also the political and social life of the country. At the outbreak of the Mutiny there were only 270 miles of railway lines in India. The only roads were military ones, beyond which there were nothing but unmetalled tracks impassable in the monsoons. Now, however, the railway mileage of India amounts to over 30,000 miles. The result is that the districts where the crop has not failed can come to the help of those that need their aid. These "great reserves of the country at large" are attracted readily to the districts which need them by the ordinary economic force of a rise in price. One of the remarkable features of the famines which have occurred since 1896 has been the slightness of the differences in the price of food all over the country.

Nevertheless, although the problem is soluble, it still remains one of intolerable difficulty. This is due to the enormous numbers that have to be relieved at the same time. These numbers have, on one occasion, reached a total of six and a half million persons. Thus we are brought back to the cry for the development of Indian manufactures. It is claimed that India, more than other countries, needs diversity of industry. The famine problem might then be brought within manageable proportions, for the numbers confronted by starvation would not be so overwhelming. This reasoning is not confined to Indians, but has been adopted by the Government. The Famine Commissioners in the Report of 1880 laid it down that, "No remedy for present evils can be complete which does not include the introduction of a diversity of occupations through which the surplus population may be drawn from agricultural pursuits and led to find the means of subsistence in manufactures, or in some such employments." In all Government reports issued since that date this policy has been accepted. It is not surprising that, as will be seen later, the general adoption of this principle has led to the demand that it should be secured, as in other countries, by a protective tariff.

CHAPTER II

THE NATURAL RESOURCES OF INDIA

We have next to inquire what are the special difficulties which confront India in her efforts to build up her manufactures. We shall thus be in a position to discuss whether these difficulties will be increased or reduced by protection and preferences. The question whether India will succeed in becoming an industrial country will be largely determined not by the acts of man, but by the gifts of Nature. We must, therefore, first examine her natural resources.

Coal.—This is the mineral most essential to India, and fortunately its production shows, up to the present, the best record of expansion. The coal-bearing strata, lying chiefly in the central districts of the peninsula, cover about 35,000 square miles. This is not a very extensive area, considering the vast size of India, but within this area the coal is by no means poor. The output during the last ten years has increased steadily from 4,600,000 tons in 1898 to 11,200,000 tons in 1907.[1] These figures may appear insignificant compared to those of Great Britain, but they mean that India now produces for herself practically all the coal that she uses. Its importance to Indian manufacture can be estimated from the fact that the great jute industry of Bengal, in spite of its overwhelming natural advantages in possessing the practical monopoly of raw jute, remained undeveloped until the opening up of the Bengal coal-field. About 90 per cent. of the Indian coal comes from this one field. The smallness of the area from which the supply comes is a grave defect, as the cost of carriage from Bengal to distant parts of India is heavy. The essential fact, however, remains that for a considerable period in the future India can rely upon the supreme advantage of indigenous coal.

[1] "Statistical Abstract for British India for 1908," p. 260.

Iron and Steel.—Proceeding to the other fundamental minerals, the story of India's production of iron is one of many vicissitudes. Her manufactures of steel and wrought iron had reached high perfection at least two thousand years ago. The famous iron pillar at Delhi, which is certainly fifteen hundred years old, is still a marvel to those who see it, and consists of a mass of wrought iron which, within modern times, could only have been produced by the largest factories. The Damascus blades were fashioned from iron brought from a remote Indian village which has now passed into obscurity. Indian steel was at one time used for cutlery, even in England. Yet at the present moment there is, in a commercial sense, nothing but the beginnings of an iron industry. There seem to have been two causes of its disappearance. The first was that by the time that India had to face the competition of modern systems of production the methods which had created the iron pillar at Delhi had been lost. The other cause recalls the history of the trade in England. Indian furnaces always used charcoal. This was very expensive, and the Indian trade died out, as the English one was in danger of doing during the seventeenth century, on account of the scarcity of the same fuel. At the present time, however, high hopes are being felt for the future of the industry. As in England it was saved by coal, so in India there is every prospect that it will be revived by the opening of the Bengal coal-fields. There is a great abundance of iron ore, while limestone and fireclay usually accompany the coal formations. The failure of a number of undertakings during the last half-century has taught Indian capitalists the lesson that success can only be achieved by a firm which commands vast capital and undertakes all processes up to the finished steel. The recently established Tata works, the greatest single enterprise in India, fulfil these conditions. Their fate will do much to determine the progress of Indian industry in the near future.

These are the fundamental minerals, and the others can be considered more shortly. Sir V. Ball points out in "The Economic Geology of India" that "were India wholly isolated from the rest of the world or were her mineral productions protected from competition, there cannot be the least doubt that she would be able, from within her own boundary, to supply very nearly all the requirements, in so far as mineral wealth is concerned, of a civilised community." Nevertheless it will be seen that at present India derives from her own soil only a very small part of the minerals that she needs.

PETROLEUM. — This industry requires special consideration, as it might play a considerable part in any manipulation of tariffs. Its development during the last ten years has been more rapid than that of any other Indian mineral industry. The production has risen from 19,000,000 gallons in 1898 to 152,000,000 gallons in 1907, an increase of 800 per cent. Almost the whole supply comes from Burmah, and the remainder from Assam. The impetus to the trade was given by the annexation of Burmah, as a result of which the methods of the hereditary oil diggers were supplanted by those of the Burmah Oil Company. In spite, however, of the progress made, India still imports mineral oil to a total value more than twice as great as that of her own output. If, therefore, the sources of the supply hold good, there are great possibilities of expansion at the expense chiefly of Russia and the United States.[1]

MANGANESE.—Sixteen years ago no manganese was produced in India. To-day in her production of this metal she stands second in the world. In spite of this position, however, the smallness of the industry is indicated by the fact that only about 7,000 men are employed in quarrying the ore.[2]

[1] See "Statistical Abstract for British India for 1908," pp. 149, 260.

[2] "Statistical Abstract for British India for 1908," p. 260.

Mica.—In the production of this mineral India is first among nations, and is responsible for more than half the world's supply. Again, however, the fact that only 10,000 men are employed in mining it should prevent any exaggerated ideas of its importance.[1] The future of this industry depends largely upon the enterprise of those who control it. The system of working in Bengal still remains primitive, the best veins are being exhausted, and modern methods will have to be introduced if the remaining veins are to be profitably exploited.

Saltpetre.—At one time India was the chief source of the world's supply of this mineral, and, as it was an essential element of gunpowder, it gave the country a peculiar political importance. Other explosive compounds, however, have now been discovered, and the potassic nitrate of India has been largely displaced by the sodic nitrate of Chili. The result is that though it still employs

[1] "Statistical Abstract for British India for 1908," p. 260.

50,000 men,[1] the production and exports of it show a tendency to diminish.[2] Its prospects depend largely upon the possibility of turning it to its natural use as a fertiliser. Experiments in this direction are being made by the Agricultural Department. If they are successful the future is assured, for the conditions for its production in Behar, from which almost all of it comes, are pronounced by geologists to be ideal.[3]

SALT.—It is very unlikely that this article would be selected either for protection or a preference. As it is a necessity which enters into the daily consumption of the mass of the people, any increase in the duty on it which was not essential for revenue would be regarded with the utmost hostility. Between a fourth and a third of the salt

[1] "Statistical Abstract for British India for 1908," p. 258.

[2] See (1) "Financial and Commercial Statistics of British India for 1907," p. 458; (2) "Statistical Abstract for British India for 1908," p. 156.

[3] See "The Development of the Mineral Resources of India," a paper to the Benares Industrial Conference, 1905 (Indian Press, Allahabad).

consumed in India is imported. The imports are chiefly to Bengal and Burmah.[1] Bengal at one time produced salt for itself, but it is at a disadvantage owing to the dampness ot the climate and the amount of fresh water discharged into the Bay of Bengal from the Ganges and the Brahmaputra. Cheshire supplies Bengal with nearly half its salt. Import and excise duties are already levied on this article, and furnish a revenue which has varied during the last ten years from four million to six million pounds.

COPPER.—Not an ounce of this metal is produced at present, but we include it in the survey because it illustrates a very important factor in the prospects of Indian industry. Many chemical industries are only rendered profitable by the utilisation of by-products. Copper smelting furnishes an example. Copper ores occur in India in large quantities and were once extensively smelted. Several attempts to revive the industry have

1 "Financial and Commercial Statistics of British India for 1907," p. 38.

been made where the lodes were reputed to be rich. The lodes have not been disappointing, and yet the endeavours have failed. The reason is that no attempt has been made to utilise the copper sulphides, whereas elsewhere the ores have only been worked successfully by the sale of these by-products. In England, for example, during the last seventy years the price of sulphuric acid has been reduced to about one-sixth of its previous level. The difficulty in India is that there are not enough local industries which demand sulphuric acid. In order, again, that such industries should be established, others which demand their by-products must also be present. Hence chemical and metallurgical industries need to exist in family groups. The group is gradually being completed in India. The development of industries connected with cotton, jute, and paper forms a market for chemical by-products. The increase of bleaching works, for example, raises the demand for sulphuric acid and soda ash. In the chemical and metallurgical industries of India, therefore, after a certain stage is reached, the expansion may be unexpectedly rapid.

The remaining minerals of India are tin, graphite, rubies, jade and gold. The production of tin and graphite, however, is so insignificant, that it does not merit a special description.[1] Rubies are, at present, the most profitable of Burmese minerals next to petroleum. The Burmese Ruby Mines Company has had a chequered career, but since new conditions were introduced into its lease in 1899, it has become more prosperous. The rubies produced in 1907 were worth £115,000.[2] Burmah is also the centre for jade. The production is increasing gradually, and in 1907 its value reached £74,000.[3] The Mysore gold mines, from which almost the whole of the Indian supply

[1] See "Financial and Commercial Statistics of British India for 1907," pp. 456, 458.

[2] "Statistical Abstract for British India, 1908," p. 261.

[3] "Statistical Abstract for British India for 1908," p. 260.

is derived, are well known on stock exchanges; but this commodity is not of importance to the subject that we have to consider.

Our review will have made it clear that, comparing the mineral wealth of India with the vast area over which it is distributed, she has not been as richly endowed as Great Britain. Her geographical position is not so favourable for international trade as it at first sight appears to be. She possesses a vast extent of sea-board, but it contains only five good harbours, and on the west coast the monsoons beat furiously from July to September. It is difficult to believe that she can ever become a great manufacturing nation in the British sense of the term, or that the average wealth of her population can approach that of the people of these islands. This conclusion, however, is not a depressing one. She can secure a reasonable diversity of industries and a large enough manufacturing population to form a fertile soil for new ideas without becoming so entirely urbanised as Great Britain. Nature, moreover, has endowed her with a climate which should enable her people to lead a full and worthy life with much less wealth than is necessary in our own country.

CHAPTER III

A SURVEY OF INDIAN INDUSTRIES

Any discussion of the proper fiscal system for India to adopt must take into account the actual industries at present existing, and examine the effect of various tariff proposals upon them. This involves a knowledge of the main features of their position. These features we shall describe now in order to avoid over-burdening the discussion when we reach the actual schemes to be examined. A part of our work has been already accomplished in the review of the mineral resources of India.

India is still witnessing the struggle, in England almost past, between the factory system and the system by which the artisan works in his own home. In cotton weaving, for example, the weaver working at home with a loom very little better than that which was used hundreds of years ago, still holds his own tenaciously against the Bombay mill equipped with the latest machinery from Lancashire. The same conflict is being waged in silk weaving, dyeing, tanning, boot and shoe manufacture, oil pressing, and rice cleaning and husking—in fact throughout the whole range of Indian manufactures. In England it has been long decided in favour of the factory system. But in India the more primitive methods still hold the field. In cotton mills, for example, the number of hands employed is only a little over two hundred thousand, whereas the hand-loom weavers number over two and a half million.[1] If the cotton and jute trade be excluded, there is no factory industry throughout India which employs 20,000 hands. There is, at present, one very serious obstacle to the rapid development of a factory system. Labour is very difficult to secure. The

[1] "Statistical Abstract for British India for 1908," pp. 17, 257.

Indian labourer does not readily adapt himself to the new methods. In factories, in hand-loom workshops, and in coal mines there is the same complaint—that the wages are higher than can be earned anywhere else, and yet there is a strange unwillingness to be tempted by them. In order to induce an Indian workman to enter a factory he has to be allowed a freedom from discipline which will soften the contrast with his older methods of work. A visitor to a Bombay cotton mill at any hour of the day will find a large number of the hands smoking in the compound. The Report of the Indian Factory Labour Commission of 1908 points out that "meals are generally eaten during the working hours of the factory; the mid-day interval is sometimes devoted to sleep, and the operative leaves his work frequently throughout the day in order to eat, smoke, bathe, and so on. In the cotton textile mills in India the average operative probably spends from one and a half to two hours each day, in addition to the statutory mid-day interval, away from his work."[1]

In the same Report it was calculated that, taking the whole staff of a cotton spinning and weaving mill, one hand in Lancashire will produce more than two and a half times the output of a hand in India.[2] Similarly the average output of the workmen employed in the Indian coal mines for 1902 was 75 tons,[3] while for the rest of the British Empire it was 285 tons, or almost four times as great.

In spite of these facts, however, there is every reason to believe that the Indian operative will eventually adapt himself to modern conditions. A distinct class of factory workers, detached from the older conditions, is beginning to be formed. In some of the older mining districts, a population with mining as their caste occupation is

[1] "Report of Factory Commission, 1908," p. 20 (Government Press, Simla).

[2] Page 19 of the Report.

[3] "Imperial Gazetteer of India," Vol. III., p. 164.

being evolved. A good deal of the inefficiency in the cotton mills is undoubtedly due to the excessive hours of labour. The average in most of them at present is from thirteen to thirteen and a half hours a day. Moreover, the Factory Labour Commission pointed out that "in the latter portion of the year 1905 the Bombay mills worked for fourteen and a half hours a day. There is no guarantee that this will not recur, and we find it prevailing permanently in the mills in Agra and other industrial centres in Northern India." It is a sound instinct of self-preservation that under these conditions prompts the operative to loiter over his work. The workers in the Calcutta jute mills working short hours by shifts do not idle away time to anything like the extent noticed in Bombay. In the engineering shops throughout India, where an eight hours day is the rule, there is very little idling. The Factory Labour Commission comes to the conclusion that "where the hours are short and the supervision is good the operative can be trained to adopt fairly regular habits of working."[1] We may, then, expect with confidence that Indian labour will gradually adapt itself to its new tasks. Indeed, one of the witnesses before the Factory Commission considered that the Indian labourer would become a better textile operative than any in the world, except the Lancashire mill hand. The important fact, however, for our discussion is that the process must be a gradual one. This consideration is often neglected in the natural impatience of many Indians to force on the growth of manufactures by means of a protective tariff.

We shall now proceed to consider the industries of India one by one, and to describe the main conditions which need to be remembered in the subsequent discussion. We shall deal first with those which may be described as "mill and factory industries," although in most of them the factory system still plays only a small part.

[1] Report, p. 21.

The remainder consist of tea, coffee, sugar, indigo and tobacco, which may be classified as "industries connected with agriculture."

COTTON SPINNING AND WEAVING.—It has already been explained that, although this is the premier mill industry in India, more than nine-tenths of the cotton weavers are still "home-workers." Many of those who wish to preserve them from being crushed out by the factories are trying to devise improved hand looms to displace their present exceedingly primitive contrivances.

It can be predicted with confidence that these experiments will succeed. It is not unlikely, however, that the effects of this success will be the opposite of those intended. A new competitor, the hand-loom factory, is now entering the field. This is an example of "the workshop system," which in Great Britain still competes with the factory system in the clothing trade, boot and shoe making, and other industries. In India the cheapness of labour power gives it a much greater chance of holding its own in the conflict with steam than it has in England. Improved hand looms will stimulate hand-loom factories as much as they will the weaver in his own home. These factories, with the advantage of collective production, may prove to be yet another fact tending to drive the old hand-loom weaver out of existence. Already young men are being urged to embark on the new system.[1] The need of India at the present juncture in her development is that her sons should devote themselves to commerce instead of crowding into professions already overstocked. Hand-loom factories offer an opportunity for young Indians to prove their mettle. The capital required is small, and to increase it beyond a narrow limit will bring no corresponding advantage. This field is not, therefore, likely to attract British firms, which usually prefer to work on a large scale.

These, however, are speculations. When we turn to the mill industry we find a record

[1] See Morison's "Indian Industrial Organisation," p. 184.

of accomplished results. Forty years ago there were only thirteen cotton mills in India, while at present there are 217.[1] The progress has been steady and continuous. This is the more creditable as the trade has met with a number of reverses which were no fault of its own. Within the last few years, for example, it has suffered from the effects of famine and from one of the fiercest plagues of modern times, which almost stopped the working of the mills. Yet throughout the years that these calamities were occurring the capital invested in the industry was steadily increasing. Another feature which is a cause of legitimate pride is that, in contrast to the jute trade, it is a truly "swadeshi" industry, for the capital and management are chiefly in Indian hands. Three-fourths of the production issues from Bombay, the home of native enterprise. There is still, however, a large home market to be captured, as the Indian

[1] "Statistical Abstract for British India for 1908," p. 257.

output amounts to only about a quarter of the imports. The chief weakness is in the production of the higher counts of yarn. But the outlook is promising, for the production of yarn is steadily rising, and this increase is due mainly to the growth in the counts above twenty.[1] The future of the industry largely depends upon whether it is possible to introduce a high class of raw cotton into India. Although the area under this crop is steadily expanding,[2] the cotton is of low grade and short in the staple. The results of the experiments of the Bombay Government in the introduction of Egyptian cotton into Sind will mean much to the future of the trade.

JUTE.—We proceed to the only other great mill industry that India possesses. Bengal is the home of the jute trade. Unlike the cotton trade, the bulk of the capital and the management is in British hands,

[1] "Statistical Abstract for British India for 1908," p. 257.

[2] "Statistical Abstract for British India for 1908," p. 123.

although lately the proportion of Indian capital has been increasing. Here again the conflict between the artisan and the factory systems is to be witnessed; but in this case the victory of the factories is almost complete. Their progress has been as uninterrupted as that of the cotton mills. The number of persons employed has risen during the last ten years from 95,000 in 1897 to 167,000 in 1906.[1] At the same time it should be pointed out that progress would have been difficult to avoid. The industry has no severe competition to face in the Indian market, while there have been no outside causes of disturbance such as have harassed the cotton industry in Bombay. Most important of all, Bengal has a monopoly of the world's supply of raw jute. With all these advantages, it is probable that Calcutta will ultimately hold the world's markets in the coarser kinds of manufacture.[2] One

[1] "Statistical Abstract for British India for 1908," p. 257.

[2] During the last nine years the value of the exports rose from £4,000,000 in 1897—8 to £10,500,000 in

danger, however, looms ahead. The fact that all the raw jute of the world is found in Bengal indicates that the supply of it is not very great. Even during the last few years there has been a significant rise in its price, and if this were to continue other fibres could be substituted for the purposes now fulfilled by jute. These facts will be of great importance when we discuss the subject of export duties.

We have now considered the only important factory industries in India. Those to which we proceed may contain great possibilities, but their present scale is insignificant.

TANNING AND LEATHER MANUFACTURES.—These should be among the most flourishing of Indian industries, for their natural advantages are unusual. India produces quantities of raw hides and skins. The skins are of the best quality, but the proportion of first-class hides is not so great. Her supply of

1906—7. A part of this increase is accounted for by a rise in price. But if instead of values the quantities of jute bags and jute cloth are considered the growth is nearly as great.—"Statistical Abstract for British India for 1908," pp. 154, 156, 184.

the other necessary materials—acacia pods, bark, cutch, Indian sumach, tanner's cassia, mangroves, and myriabolams—is also excellent. Yet her exports of tanned hides and skins are small and practically stationary,[1] while, on the other hand, those of raw hides and skins are great and have more than doubled in the last nine years.[2] The explanation is to be found in the notorious crudity of the methods of tanning. Again we come upon the conflict between the artisan and the factory systems, but here the older system holds the greater part of the field. Village tanners yearly convert vast quantities of fairly good hides into inferior leather. The annual waste of materials for which they are responsible represents a loss of hundreds of thousands of pounds.

[1] The exports of tanned hides and skins amounted to a value of £2,500,000 in 1897—8, and nine years later (in 1906—7) to £2,900,000.—"Statistical Abstract for British India for 1908," p. 187.

[2] The exports of raw hides and skins have increased during the last nine years from a value of £3,000,000 in 1897 to over £7,000,000 in 1906—7.—"Statistical Abstract for British India for 1908," p. 187.

Tanneries of the factory type have, however, made their appearance, chiefly in Madras, and are beginning to supplant the indigenous ones. In 1906 they employed 10,000 men.[1] Even these, however, have no great reputation for enterprise.[2] We shall recur to these facts when we consider the claim that Indian industries cannot develop without a protective tariff.

For the same reason that we should expect a flourishing tanning industry we should also look for large leather manufacture. A considerable internal demand is growing up for cheap machine-made boots and shoes, but it is met by an increase of imports. The factory system is still in its infancy. Even the factories which exist are largely dependent upon the support of the military and other Government departments. Cawnpore is the headquarters of the modern manufacture of

[1] "Statistical Abstract for British India for 1908," p. 258.

[2] See "Chrome Tanning in Madras," by Mr. Alfred Chatterton, Director of Industries in Madras, a paper read before the Calcutta Conference in 1906.

boots and shoes, saddlery, trunks, and military equipment. On the other hand, there are immense local manufactures of boots and shoes under the older system. Almost every village has its shoemaker, while in the larger towns the trade occupies entire streets.

SILK MILLS.—The competition between the different methods of production is clearly shown in silk weaving. The home workers, with one or two looms, still represent the dominant system, and are to be found all over the country. The beginnings of a factory system, of which Bombay seems likely to be the centre, are to be seen in four large silk mills worked by steam power. The workshop system is represented by about thirty hand-loom factories (most of them in Bengal), which do not employ European machinery. In spite of the high skill of the Indian weavers the industry is losing ground. The exports of silk manufactures have shown a continuous decline during the last decade,[1]

[1] The value of the exports has diminished from £86,000 in 1897—8 to £45,500 in 1906—7.—"Statistical Abstra t for British India for 1908," p. 155.

while the imports are rapidly increasing.[1] Silk filatures also show a tendency to decline in numbers.[2]

Woollen Mills. — There are only six woollen mills throughout India, and the trade shows no signs of expansion. Even the existing mills produce chiefly for the army and the police. Yet the demand for woollen goods in India is appreciable. The imports are increasing rapidly.[3]

Paper Mills.—This industry is in much the same position as the woollen trade. There are eight mills in India, and the trade gives little indication of growth.[4] The Government supports the existing mills by obtaining from them most of the foolscap,

[1] The imports of "piece goods" and "mixed" have increased from 14,000,000 yards in 1897—8 to 20,500,000 yards in 1906—7.—"Statistical Abstract for British India," p. 150.

[2] "Imperial Gazetteer of India," Vol. III., p. 209; and "Statistical Abstract for British India for 1908," p. 250.

[3] During the last nine years their value has increased from £750,000 in 1897—8 to £1,350,000 in 1906—7.

[4] "Statistical Abstract for British India for 1908," p. 258.

blotting paper, note paper and envelopes required for the public offices. The trade has every opportunity for expansion, as is shown by the fact that the imports have doubled within the last nine years.[1] Until the industry adopts more modern methods and materials it cannot hold its own against the cheap wood pulp paper imported from Europe.

The remaining industries which come within the category with which we are at present dealing do not deserve any detailed description, either because tariffs will not affect them, or because they are only represented by one or two firms. They consist of iron and brass foundries, railway works, breweries, dyeing works, chemical works, tile factories, rice mills, cotton ginning and cleaning mills, lace factories, soap works, pottery works, aluminium works, printing

[1] The imports of paper and pasteboard have increased from £220,000 in 1897—8 to £534,000 in 1906—7.—"Statistical Abstract for British India in 1908," p. 148.

presses, rope works, glass works, works for the production of matches, umbrellas and felt caps.

We now come to the second division into which the industries of India may be classified—those connected with agriculture. The industries coming under this head consist of sugar, indigo, coffee, tea, and tobacco. As each of these might play a considerable part in any scheme of tariffs, they require careful examination.

SUGAR. — The history of this industry during the last few years is full of surprises, which are by no means creditable to the Indian producers. The consumption of sugar in India is rapidly increasing. Yet the area under cultivation is stationary with a tendency to diminish,[1] while the imports are increasing rapidly so as to capture the expanding Indian market.[2] The explanation

[1] The areas under cultivation during the last nine years have diminished from 2,648,000 acres in 1897—8 to 2,623,000 acres in 1906—7.—"Statistical Abstract for British India for 1908," p. 123.

[2] The imports have increased during the last nine

at one time appeared simple. The foreign bounties given to beet sugar were held to be responsible. The Government of India therefore passed the Countervailing Sugar Duties Act of 1899, by which, in addition to the ordinary duty, a special duty was imposed in the case of bounty-fed sugar, of the same amount as the bounty. This counterstroke was expected to revive the Indian production, but the imports, instead of declining, went on increasing more rapidly than before.[1] Again the explanation appeared easy. The foreign manufacturers were now bringing into play cartel bounties, by which the advantage secured to them in their home markets by their high import duties was used for assisting the sale of the sugar abroad.

years from the value of £3,200,000 in 1897—8 to £5,800,000 in 1906—7.—"Statistical Abstract for British India for 1908," p. 149.

[1] Value of imports of sugar, 1890—1900, £2,250,000 (countervailing duties imposed); value of imports of sugar 1900—1, £3,700,700; 1901—2, £3,900,000.—"Statistical Abstract for British India for 1908," p. 183.

Again the Government stepped in and imposed further countervailing duties. Nevertheless, the imports still continued to increase, and are now higher than ever before, while throughout the period the home production has remained stationary.[1] How can these results be explained? The failure of the Indian industry to take advantage of its opportunities is due not to causes which tariffs can cure, but to its own notorious want of enterprise. On the other hand, the beet sugar manufacturers have not relied upon their bounties. Those who ascribe their progress to bounties alone should remember that by scientific work the sugar which the beetroot yielded has been increased from 9 per cent. to 16 or 18 per cent. The best machinery has been adopted for extracting the sugar; chemical processes obtain the last traces of crystallisable sugar

[1] Value of imports of sugar 1902—3, £3,300,000; 1903—4, £4,000,000; 1904—5, £4,600,000; 1905—6, £5,200,000; 1906—7, £5,800,000.—"Statistical Abstract for British India for 1908," p. 183.

from the molasses; and the waste products—at one time a positive expense—are converted into salts of potash, ammonia, and other valuable chemical products.[1] The Indian industry is now demanding protection, but the best remedy for its misfortunes will be to accept the warning of the Surat Industrial Conference that "it is absolutely necessary to encourage the cultivation of healthier and more prolific varieties of cane, to employ greater care in cultivation, to use more economical processes for extracting the juice, and above all to adopt the most modern and efficient methods of refining."[2]

INDIGO.—This industry presents a gloomy picture, but not, as in the case of sugar, through faults of its own. Indian vegetable colours have for centuries held a foremost place in the markets of the world, but again

[1] See a paper on "The Development of the Mineral Resources of India," read to the Benares Industrial Conference, 1903, by Sir Thomas Holland (Nateson & Co., Madras).

[2] Resolution 7 of the Surat Industrial Conference, 1907 (Nateson & Co., Madras).

we are met by the competition between the older methods and the results of modern science. The story of the extraction of a wonderful colouring material from coal tar is one of the romances of modern industry. The effect of the competition of this new product is seen from the fact that the area under indigo in India at present has shrunk to less than one-third the area of nine years ago.[1]

The committee appointed in 1900 did not conceal its view that the days of the industry were numbered. "Without taking too pessimistic a view of the future of indigo, it is reasonable to anticipate that the competition of synthetic indigo will prevent any future increase in the price of vegetable indigo, that it will soonest and most injuriously affect the finest and most expensive indigo, which is that of Behor, and cause a further reduction of price which would hardly clear

[1] In 1897—8 the area under indigo was 1,400,000 acres; by 1906—7 it was reduced to 450,000 acres.—"Statistical Abstract for India in 1908," p. 123.

the planter in a good season, while a bad season would be ruinous to him. In the end—though we trust the end is a long way off—the competition of synthetic indigo may bring about the supersession of vegetable indigo, as the competition of alizarine dyes ended in the supersession of madder." [1]

In spite of these facts, however, in the publication expressing the "Views of the Government of India on the Question of Preferential Tariffs," we find in the memorandum of Sir Edward Law, the Finance Minister, the following statement:—"If the United Kingdom were to impose a reasonable duty on synthetic indigo whilst admitting natural indigo free, the difficulties of our indigo planters would disappear as by magic."[2] This is an example of the lack of perspective which expects very large results from very small causes.

[1] See the "Decennial Statement exhibiting the Moral and Material Progress of India," p. 332, issued in 1903.

[2] See p. 21 of the publication.

Tea.—We now come to an industry whose future is full of hope, and whose growth during the last generation has been remarkable.[1] The expansion, in fact, was so rapid as to lead to a fall in prices which involved the trade in great difficulties. The difficulties were in this case a stimulus to progress, and vigorous efforts to push the sale of Indian tea were undertaken. For this purpose a small duty on tea has been imposed, and the proceeds of it are used by a representative committee to open up new markets.

Large plantations have been established, and machinery has taken the place of manual labour. One result has been that the freedom of Indian tea from the adulteration and impurity incidental to Asiatic hand labour has enabled it practically to oust Chinese tea from the British market. Ninety per cent. of the tea imported into the United

[1] In 1885 the area under tea in India was 440 square miles. By 1903, a little less than twenty years later, it had increased to 820 square miles.

Kingdom in 1907 came from India and Ceylon, while only 3 per cent. came from China. We shall return to these facts when we are considering the proposals that Great Britain should grant a preference to Indian tea.

COFFEE.—The prospects of this industry are by no means so bright as those of tea. There is only a small home demand for it, while the foreign markets have been devastated by the competition of the cheap Brazilian product. The average London price sank, for example, from 101*s*. per cwt. in 1894 to 47*s*. per cwt. in 1901.[1] The effect of this competition is shown by the steady decrease of the area under coffee.[2] We shall indicate later that this seems to be an industry to which a preference in the British markets might be of some real assistance.

[1] See the "Decennial Statement exhibiting the Moral and Material Progress of India" for 1903, p. 233.

[2] This has shrunk during the last nine years from 151 acres in 1897—8 to 96 acres in 1906—7.—"Statistical Abstract for British India for 1908," p. 122.

Tobacco.—The area under tobacco has remained stationary during the last nine years at about a million acres.[1] The exports are increasing steadily.[2] It has, moreover, a considerable prospect of an expanding home consumption. Indians, in many parts, smoke from early youth, but the "hukka" is gradually being abandoned for cigars and cigarettes. These are imported in great quantities, and the prospects of the Indian tobacco industry depend largely upon its success in taking their place. The exports to Great Britain are, at present, insignificant,[3] a fact which is of importance in the discussion of preferences.

[1] "Statistical Abstract for British India for 1908," p. 123.

[2] The value of the exports has risen from £197,000 in 1897—8 to £206,000 in 1906—7.—"Statistical Abstract for British India for 1908," p. 123.

[3] See "Annual Statement of the Sea-borne Trade and Navigation of British India for 1907," Vol. I., pp. 441, 442.

CHAPTER IV

SWADESHI AND THE DEMAND FOR PROTECTION IN INDIA

PUBLIC opinion in India is overwhelmingly protectionist. If she were granted her fiscal freedom there is no doubt that she would use it to erect a high tariff which from the nature of her trade would be directed chiefly against British goods. Among the educated and commercial classes free trade is regarded as a policy forced upon India against her best interests by Great Britain. Those who sympathise with the reasons given in the first chapter for building up manufactures will not be surprised at this attitude. The latest expression of it is to be found in the Swadeshi movement. This has received the support of "moderates," "extremists," the business community consisting of non-political men, and even of the Government.

As the term, however, is used in more than one sense, an explanation of its real significance is needed. Swadeshi means strictly "my own country." This spirit chiefly manifests itself in practice by the purchase of home-made articles in preference to foreign ones. Swadeshi, therefore, is voluntary protection. It seeks to secure by the willing action of patriotic purchasers what nations with their fiscal freedom secure by means of protective tariffs. The fact that Indians of all shades of thought are unanimous in accepting this doctrine indicates the strength of the protectionist sentiment. As British observers do not often have the opportunity of hearing the views of representative Indians in their own words, we quote a number of the statements of the Swadeshi principle from various schools of Indian thought.

The point of view of those who are interested in economic rather than in political questions is best expressed by the Industrial Conference which meets annually.

We therefore select the passages bearing on this subject from the presidential address delivered at the last three sessions of the Conference.

Mr. Romesh Chunder Dutt, the most copious writer on Indian economics, pointed out in the presidential address at Benares in 1905 that British politicians were themselves advocates of the Swadeshi principle:—"The Swadeshi movement is one which all nations on earth are seeking to adopt in the present day. Mr. Chamberlain is seeking to adopt it by a system of protection. Mr. Balfour seeks to adopt it by a scheme of retaliation. France, Germany, and the United States and all the British colonies adopt it by building up a wall of prohibitive duties. We have no control over our fiscal legislation; and we adopt the Swadeshi scheme, therefore, by a laudable resolution to use our home manufactures, as far as practicable, in preference to foreign manufactures. If we succeed in this noble endeavour, we shall present to the world an instance unparalleled in the history of modern times of a nation protecting its manufactures and industries without protective duties."

Sir Vibhaldas Damodar Thackersey, a prominent Bombay business man, presided over the next Conference, held in Calcutta in 1906. He also pointed out that Swadeshi was not peculiar to India. "Swadeshism is enforced in many civilised countries by means of prohibitive tariffs and bounties to home producers. We are only following the example of these nations by making voluntary efforts to encourage indigenous industries. There is nothing wrong in this. On the contrary, it is all the more creditable to us that what in other countries requires to be enforced by the State is undertaken here by the spontaneous action of the people."

Similarly, Dewan Bahadur Ambalal Desai, the President of the third Conference, held at Surat in 1907, argued as follows: "The protection of new or nascent industries by means of high import duties and by bounties is held to be allowable by some of the highest authorities of the Free Trade school. If the State in India had been identified in economic interests with the Indian people, some measure of protection might have been adopted by it long ago. But the Government in India being the representative in India of free trade, Britain is not at liberty, at present, to afford economic protection in any form to Indian industries. The people of India ought, therefore, to step into the vacuum and do by voluntary protection what the State might have achieved in an easier way by tariffs and bounties."

Turning to the leaders of political thought, M. G. K. Gokhale, the leader of the Indian "moderates," bases his defence of Swadeshi on the orthodox argument from "infant industries": "By ensuring the consumption of indigenous articles in their early stage, when their quality is inferior and their price is higher, or when they labour under both these disadvantages, we can do for our industries what protectionist Governments have done for theirs by means of State protection. . . . In course of time the quality of Swadeshi articles is bound to improve and their cost of production to become less and less."[1] Finally, M. Tilak, the leader of the "extremists," speaking at the Indian National Congress of 1906 in Calcutta, argued in much the same spirit that, "since this Government is not going to stop the drain by imposing a protective duty, it becomes imperatively necessary to adopt a measure by which we can do ourselves what the Government ought to have done long ago."

While in this way Swadeshi encourages home producers, it at the same time enjoins upon them the need of rising to their opportunities. We have pointed out, and shall have to do so again, that the essential weakness of Indian industry is the lack of

[1] From an address at Lucknow in 1907. See "Speeches of the Hon. M. G. K. Gokhale, C.I.E.," p. 818 (Nateson & Co., Madras).

initiative. Swadeshi preaches the courage and mutual confidence which will enable Indians to strike out fresh paths for themselves. Although many of the enterprises started under its stimulus have failed, and doubtless will fail, the first step towards overcoming a fault is to recognise its existence.

Swadeshi also claims that it will offer those who are still too poor and ignorant to understand the larger problems of political life the opportunity of doing something for their country, and of thus beginning to feel the spirit of nationalism. This has been well expressed by the great Bengalee orator, Surendranath Banerjee: "The Deccan peasant or the Bengalee rustic may find some difficulty in understanding the merits of a system of representative government. The subtleties of the question involved in the separation of judicial from executive functions may elude the grasp of his untrained mind. But when you tell him that the wealth of the country must be kept in the country, that it is to his advantage that it should be so kept, and that for this purpose he must purchase country-made articles in preference to foreign articles, he opens wide his eyes and ears and drinks in the lesson."[1]

So far all Indian thinkers are agreed. Our purpose, which is merely to illustrate the strength of the protectionist sentiment in India, does not necessitate entering deeply into the later developments of Swadeshi. For the sake of clearness, however, a few words with regard to them may be useful. A section of Indian opinion took up the Swadeshi movement as a means of inflicting injury on Great Britain. It was argued that only by this method could British people be roused into taking an interest in India, and listening to her complaints. The following statement of this position was given by Mr. Lajpat Rai:—

"The British people are not a spiritual

[1] Speech before the Swadeshi Vastu Pracharini Sabha, Bombay, 1906. See "Swadeshi Movement," p. 20 (Nateson & Co., Madras).

people. They are either a fighting race or a commercial people. It will be like throwing pearls before swine to appeal to them in the name of higher morality, or justice, or on ethical grounds. They are a self-reliant, haughty people who can appreciate self-respect and self-reliance even in their opponents. It is, then, for the Indians to decide whether they mean to continue to appeal to them in the name of political justice and fair play, or whether they intend to attract their attention to the existing intolerable condition of things in India by inflicting losses in business and by adopting an attitude of retaliatory self-reliance."[1]

Such a policy as this is not easily distinguished from "boycott." So it came about that among a certain section Swadeshi came to mean abstention from British goods in particular rather than from foreign goods in general. The next step was equally easy. The boycott of British goods was extended, on the model of the Senn Fein policy in

[1] From the *Indian Review*.

Ireland, to the boycott of all British institutions. This was the policy which finally led the Indian National Congress to break up in uproar at Surat. The "moderates" insisted on confining the Swadeshi movement to its original purpose of protection. As President of the Congress in 1905, M. Gokhale had already pointed out that "the term 'boycott' has got unsavoury associations, and it conveys to the mind before anything else a vindictive desire to injure another. Such a desire on our part, as a normal feature of our relations with England, is out of the question."

As a result of the disgraceful scenes of violence at Surat, the Indian National Congress has been reconstituted. All delegated have now to sign a declaration which excludes the "extremist" section. The latter party have found the ground cut away from under their feet by the reforms initiated by Lord Morley. Swadeshi in future will therefore revert to its original meaning, and "boycott" is not likely to be much heard of further.

The argument for protection in India is now easy to state. It is in fact contained in what has already been written. In the first chapter it was explained that there is one conclusion which forms a common ground for all schools of thought in India, from "extremists" to the Government—that the manufactures of the country must be built up. The arguments by which this view is supported are similar to those used by Alexander Hamilton and List. The future of India depends upon her power to assimilate Western ideas and scientific methods. This power will not be easily acquired by a people who are almost entirely agricultural. Progress comes from the towns, for in them active social intercourse and the contact of mind with mind create mental keenness and adaptability. The Government lays more emphasis upon the purely economic reason. If a large proportion of the agricultural population can be diverted into manufactures, it will be easier for future administrators to grapple with the awful problem of famine. The question then arises as to how the manufactures are to be created. The answer in India is the same as in all other countries in an apparently similar position. While they are "infant industries" they need the shelter of protective tariffs. After they have secured the advantages of production on a large scale, they will be able to stand upon their own feet.

CHAPTER V

AN EXAMINATION OF INDIAN PROTECTIONISM

It must not be imagined that the discussion on which we are about to enter is of merely academic interest. If protection for the United Kingdom is within the range of practical politics, protection for India is in the same position, for, as will be explained later, the one will certainly lead to the other.[1]

A discussion of Indian protectionism must start from certain generally accepted truths which here must be merely stated. The reader who wishes to examine them further will find them explained at length in any text-book of economics. An industry which secures protection obtains the right of levying a tribute upon the community. It is enabled to increase the price of its product

[1] See pp. 96—101.

and so to lay a burden on the consuming public. The argument that this does not happen, because the protective duty is paid by the foreign producer, will not bear examination. If the foreign manufacturer pays the duty and sends the goods at the same price as before, there is no advantage to the industry which is being protected. If it was being undersold before, and the price is not raised, it is being undersold still, and the protective duty has failed in its object. Protection therefore can only be effective in so far as it raises prices.[1] Whatever efforts may be made to escape from this conclusion during mere arguments, its truth is always tacitly accepted when the practical business of devising a tariff has to be faced. In the

[1] No economist would deny that there are certain cases in which protective tariffs fall, to a greater or less extent, upon the foreign producer, and that therefore the prices are not raised to the full extent of the duty. These instances are of importance when duties for revenue are being considered. But they are not of importance when duties for protective purposes are under consideration, because in this case, in so far as they fail to raise prices, they fail to give protection.

existing Indian tariff, for example, coal, raw wool, raw cotton, wood pulp, machinery, and many other articles are placed upon a free list. The reason is, of course, that it is taken for granted that an import duty will raise their price, and they are too important to other industries to permit this to occur. For the same reason iron, steel, and many articles made from them are admitted at nominal duties.

The chief remaining argument in the armoury of popular protectionism is that it "gives employment." This doctrine is, of course, recognised as a fallacy by all instructed opinion. Nevertheless its hold upon the public mind is so powerful that it has swept before it the democracies of all countries except the United Kingdom. In India, however, its foolishness ought to be plainly evident. There is no need to "give employment," for the industries of the country are already crying for labour which they cannot obtain.

Indian protectionists do not deny the

truth of these arguments. Their answer to them is that they only ask that their industries should be protected during their "infant" stages. The tribute, it is argued, is worth paying for this short period, and should be regarded as an investment of capital. When the industries have grown to maturity they will be able to stand by their own strength. The country will then be repaid many times over for the tribute that has been expected from it, because a new industry will have grown up whose products the public can obtain more cheaply than if they were still dependent upon foreign supplies. This argument does not contain any such logical impossibilities as are found in the case for popular protection. Nevertheless, Indian thinkers do not yet realise how perilous it is. Infant industries do not grow to maturity. The argument has always been merely the thin end of the wedge. When it has served its purpose in overcoming the opposition to protection it has been stultified, for the industries have been treated as if they remained infants for ever. The difficulties which confront a Government which wishes to use the argument honestly are indeed overwhelming. Behind the tariff wall a number of industries establish themselves which can never, perhaps, exist without it. It is better that they should perish than live to be a burden upon the nation. But the agitation on their behalf is very strong. Similarly even those industries which can stand by themselves have become inflated beyond their natural limits. The removal of the tariff wall means the extinction of the weaker firms and a heavy blow to others. If, for example, the Indian cotton mills had obtained a protective duty of 20 per cent. twenty years ago, does anyone believe that it would have been taken away now that the industry has secured all the advantages of production on a large scale? Those who are threatened with loss form a compact interest bringing concentrated pressure to bear upon the Government. On the other hand, the interests of the public are diffused over too wide an area to be powerful as a political force. The tribute which each consumer pays is so small that it is not worth the while of any organised body to press the Government very hard. The temptation of the Government to follow the line of least resistance is increased by the fact that it has grown to depend upon the protective duties as a source of revenue. Thus one industry after another imposes a permanent burden upon the community. Finally the "infant industry" argument is forgotten, and popular protection has established itself.

When we consider the special conditions of India the dangers appear more serious still. Protection tends to sap the vitality of industry. Economic progress is dependent upon the pressure of keen competition. Industries which are in a position of unhealthy security because they are sheltered behind a tariff wall lose the spirit of improvement. The advocates of Indian protection are in the habit of pointing to the United States, Germany, and the self-governing colonies. Their position, however, does not furnish a true analogy to that of India. Each of them is a nation remarkable for the natural vigour of its people, and it is difficult for even protection to damp their energy. The position of India is exactly the opposite, for her great danger is inertia. The resources of the country are not being opened out by Indian initiative. Indian manufacturers follow faithfully in the paths already trodden by British enterprise. Everywhere there is a noticeable desire to depend upon the Government rather than upon personal effort. Indian thinkers are continually pointing out these weaknesses to their fellow-countrymen. No one insisted upon them more strongly than Justice Ranade :—

"Our habits of mind are conservative to a fault. Capital is scarce, immobile, and unenterprising. Co-operation on a large scale of either labour or capital is unknown. The desire for accumulation is very weak, peace and security having been almost unknown over large areas for any length of time till within the last century. Our laws and institutions favour a low standard of life, and encourage subdivision and not concentration of wealth. The religious ideals of life condemn the ardent pursuit of wealth as a mistake to be avoided as much as possible. These are old legends and inherited weaknesses. Stagnation and dependence, poverty and depression—these are written in broad characters on the face of the land and its people."[1]

It would be unfair to leave this subject without pointing out that these statements need not make Indian patriots too despondent. The genius of the Indian peoples has not in the past been in the direction of

[1] "Essays on Economics," p. 26.

Similarly the Gekwar of Baroda, who has earned distinction by his great interest in the commercial development of India, pointed out to the Industrial Conference at Calcutta that "the pursuit of new truth is the first concern of every stalwart mind in the West, while the mass of our people are content to live stolid conventional lives, blindly following the precepts of their fathers, rather than emulating the example they set of intellectual independence and constructive energy."

Western scientific methods. The system of caste has concentrated their best trained minds upon speculation, while industry has been regarded as an inferior calling. Providence has entrusted the British race with the task of guiding them in the unfamiliar paths of Western industry. Justice Ranade, although he was addressing his own countrymen, pointed us to a high conception of our duties: "It cannot well be a mere accident that the destinies of this country have been entrusted to the guidance of a nation whose characteristic strength is opposed to all our weaknesses, whose enterprise in commerce and manufacture knows no bounds, whose capital overflows the world, whose view of life is full of hope, and whose powers of organisation have never been surpassed."[1]

The extent to which the industries of India are controlled by her own sons will be the measure of the degree to which we have fulfilled our trust. We have no right to expect, however, that on the unfamiliar road

[1] "Essays in Economics," p. 25.

that they are now treading they should easily strike out into fresh directions. The capacity of the Indian peoples to adapt themselves to Western methods can only be judged after they have had full time to assimilate them.

We return to the question whether protection, with its demoralising effects, will furnish the most favourable influence for training the Indian peoples in their new tasks. Yet the survey that we made of the chief industries of the country showed that in most of them the greater part of the production was still carried on by obsolete methods. This conservatism is the fundamental weakness of the trade of India. If it can be overcome her industries will develop without any protective tariff quite as fast as is healthy in the present unprepared condition of her labour. Conservatism is, however, the very fault which protection is calculated to perpetuate.

We shall now take the chief industries of

[1] "Essays in Economics," p. 25.

India and examine the probable effects of protection upon each of them. The survey which has been made of the conditions of the industries renders the task an easy one. Before it can be undertaken, however, some forecast must be attempted of the probable nature of an Indian protective tariff. It could be drawn up on one of two principles. It might be either a general tariff on imports as a whole, or a special tariff for the benefit of only a few industries with peculiar claims. The foundations of a tariff on the first principle have already been laid. India possesses a general tariff of 5 per cent., which, although it has been levied for revenue, has within its limits a distinctly protective effect. Moreover, the modifications necessary to it have also been worked out. There is a free list for commodities essential to other industries, such as coal, machinery, raw cotton, cotton twist and yarn, wood pulp, raw wool, and railway materials, while on the same principle commodities almost, but not quite, as necessary, such as iron and steel, are admitted at a nominal rate.[1] A protective tariff would naturally follow the lines already laid down. The preliminary work has been accomplished, and the Government would not be willing to relinquish revenue by freeing the commodities already paying duty. An idea of the protective system which India would probably adopt can, therefore, be obtained by imagining that the duties in the existing tariff are raised from 10 to 20 per cent., and that the unpopular excise duties on cotton manufactures are repealed.

If, therefore, on the second principle, a special tariff to protect select industries is adopted, it will probably be as a supplement to the one which has just been sketched. The "infant industry" argument indeed leads to the conclusion that those nascent manufactures which give special promise of eventual success ought to be granted a special protection. At the end of the chapter we

[1] "The Statistical Abstract for British India for 1908," p. 266.

shall be able to select the industries to which the argument applies in India.

An Indian protective tariff, however, would not consist solely of import duties. India is in a specially favourable position for imposing export duties, as she produces certain commodities of which the exports are large, and of which she is the only source of supply.

An export duty has already been laid upon rice to meet the needs of Indian revenue. This, however, is by no means the most suitable article that could have been selected. At one time, perhaps, India and Burmah enjoyed something like a monopoly of its supply for the European markets. But this is no longer the case, while other grains are being substituted for rice in distillation and the manufacture of starch. On the other hand, raw jute fulfils all the conditions needed for an effective export duty. India possesses the monopoly of it, while it is the raw material of industries which compete with her own jute manufactures. As a source of revenue it should be more profitable than the duty on rice, for the value of the exports of raw jute amounted in 1906—7 to nearly £18,000,000, while that of rice reached only £12,500,000.[1] Moreover, the chief danger to the future of the jute industry is the possibility that the supply of raw jute may not prove equal to the demand for it. The price has already been rising in a significant manner. If, therefore, India were granted her fiscal freedom, it is probable that she would substitute a duty on jute for the existing one on rice. Lac and til are also commodities which suggest themselves as suitable for export duties. In 1906—7 the value of the exports of lac was £2,300,000 and of til £1,700,000.[2]

In considering the chief industries separately we shall adopt the same order as in our original survey and examine the effect of a protective system, first upon the development of India's mineral resources, next upon her manufactures, and lastly upon the

[1] "Statistical Abstract for British India for 1908," p. 155.

[2] "Statistical Abstract for British India for 1908," pp. 155, 186.

industries connected with agriculture. The minerals which were included in the survey were coal, iron and steel, petroleum, manganese, mica, saltpetre, salt, copper, tin, graphite, rubies and jade, and gold.

(1) No protection is feasible for coal, saltpetre, manganese, mica, graphite, rubies and jade, as the imports of them are either very small or non-existent. Coal, moreover, is an essential to production on which no duty would be tolerated. It is on the free list of the existing tariff. Saltpetre is a mineral of which the production certainly needs to be stimulated, as it shows a tendency to decline. The stimulus cannot, however, be applied by protection, as the imports in 1906—7 only reached a value of £50.[1]

(2) Iron and steel only pay nominal duties of 1 per cent. in the existing tariff. They are of such importance to other industries that the Indian Government has not ventured in the past to impose effective duties upon them.

[1] "Statistics of the Sea-borne Trade and Navigation of British India," 1907, Vol. I., p. 121.

It has, however, given the industry protection in the form of subsidies. If the Tata works fulfil the hopes of their founders, this policy might be revived.

(3) Salt is a necessity to the masses of the Indian peoples. It is already subject to an excise duty and to a corresponding import duty. But these are watched with the utmost vigilance, and an additional import duty for protective purposes is scarcely within the bounds of discussion.

(4) The output of tin is on too insignificant a scale to entitle it to protection, while no copper at all is produced.

(5) We are thus left with petroleum. Although its output has increased more rapidly during the last ten years than that of any other mineral product, India's imports of it are still twice as valuable as her own production.[1] A protective tariff therefore might reduce the value of these imports.

Turning to the second group, the factory

[1] Compare p. 15.

industries, the only ones which have at present reached a scale which is more than insignificant are cotton, jute and silk manufactures, tanning, boot, shoe, and leather manufacture, woollen weaving and paper-making.

In spite of the remarkable advance of the cotton trade, India still imports cotton goods to four times the value of her own output. A protective duty, therefore, might lead to an expansion of this industry.[1]

The jute manufacturers, on the other hand, have little to hope for from protection. The total value of the imports of jute goods in 1906—7 amounted to less than ninety thousand pounds.[2] As the exports for the same year amounted to ten and a half million pounds,[3] it will be seen how small a proportion of the trade would be affected by a duty.

Tanners and leather manufacturers would

[1] Compare p. 32.

[2] "Statistics for the Sea-borne Trade and Navigation of British India for 1907," Vol. I., p. 199.

[3] "Statistical Abstract for British India for 1908," p. 184.

probably insist that their "infant industries" had a special claim for protection. Our survey of their position, however, has shown that they deserve little sympathy. Nature has showered its advantages upon their trade, but they fail to rise to their opportunities. Their weakness is due to causes which protection will only encourage. We realise, however, such considerations are not likely to be taken into account when a tariff is being drawn up, and these industries would doubtless be included with the rest.

Similar reflections arise when we consider the woollen and paper mills. They already receive a species of protection, as they are largely dependent upon Government support. They would certainly claim and obtain their share of protective duties, but the methods of both are unprogressive. Silk manufactures also would doubtless be included in the general scheme, although the factory system is in its infancy and the bulk of the production is carried on by less advanced methods.

We are now left with the third group of industries: those connected with agriculture, consisting of sugar, indigo, tea, coffee, and tobacco. Those which, at first sight, have the strongest claim to protection are indigo and coffee, declining industries whose misfortunes are continually being pressed upon the public of India. But an examination of their imports proves that tariffs will be of practically no avail. India consumes only the inferior grades of indigo, and the value of the imports in 1906—7 came to only £6,500.[1] Similarly there is little demand for coffee, and in 1906—7 the imports were valued only at £18,000.[2]

The sugar planters are already demanding protection, not as part of a general scheme, but as a privilege apart from other producers. No industry deserves it less, and the demand is an attempt to throw upon the public the

[1] "Annual Statement of the Sea-borne Trade and Navigation of British India for 1907," Vol. I., p. 134.

[2] "Annual Statement of the Sea-borne Trade and Navigation for British India for 1907," Vol. I., p. 47.

penalty for the faults of the planters themselves. It has been shown that they have signally failed to take advantage of the countervailing duties which were imposed for their protection. The remedy does not lie in further protection, but in their own efforts. If, however, a general tariff is adopted, this particular industry is not likely, in the common agitation, to be excluded.

The two remaining industries are tea and tobacco. The tea planters, in contrast to the sugar planters, have equipped their estates with the most modern machinery, and by such means have already driven China tea almost entirely out of the British market. The home market also is likely to expand, since the tea-drinking habit is growing among the town populations of India. As a large part of this home market is still held by Chinese tea, a duty might lead to a further expansion of the Indian industry. The tobacco growers also might receive considerable assistance from a tariff. Vast quantities of cheap cigars and cigarettes are imported, the place of which might be taken by the products of India herself.

From this survey, it appears that the industries which a tariff might assist are those which produce iron and steel, petroleum, cotton manufactures, tanned hides and skins, leather goods, silk and woollen manufactures, paper, sugar, tea, and tobacco. The arguments of Indian protectionists, however, have no application to petroleum, cotton manufactures, sugar and tea. These are established industries already enjoying the full benefits of production on a large scale. Any advantage that they received would merely represent the proceeds of a tribute levied from the public, without thc excuse that they were in thc "infant stage." We are left, therefore, with tanned hides and skins, leather, silk and woollen manufactures, paper, tobacco, and perhaps iron and steel. These may claim to come within the category of nascent industries. If a tariff on the second principle that we described were adopted these are the trades which would be selected for it. But, as was pointed out in our survey, the tanning and leather industries are being kept back by their own inertia, while silk and woollen manufactures and paper-making also suffer from the conservatism of their methods. Protection will merely pander to these weaknesses. We are therefore reduced to tobacco and perhaps iron and steel, as the industries which emerge from our examination.

Our general conclusion is that India needs a strong free trade school among her thinkers and administrators. The tangible benefits of protection reduce themselves on examination to such small proportions that they do not justify the running the serious risks which the policy entails. Nevertheless, if India were once granted her fiscal freedom we have no doubt that protection would be adopted. The movement of opinion is already so strong, and the example of other countries whose position appears to be similar to her own is so powerful, that no arguments seem likely to hold her back. But there is no reason why the present uncritical protectionism should hold the field for want of opposition. Nowhere in the Indian literature on the subject are the weaknesses that we have been discussing emphasised. Here would be the work of a free trade school. If then a protective tariff were adopted they could free it from its worse abuses. India with her eyes open to the dangers of her course would be left with no excuse for stultifying the "infant industries" argument by allowing one trade after another to become a burden on the community. Under present conditions no industry should remain in the infant stage for more than fifteen, or at the most twenty, years. It should be clearly laid down from the beginning that this was to be the limit of the protection. India indeed may prove to be the one country strong enough to consistently carry out a policy of this kind. Her government, because it is still to a large extent absolute, can override "the clamorous importunity of partial interests" more firmly than is possible in more democratic States. If it used its strength protection would be robbed of many of its possibilities of evil.

CHAPTER VI

THE POSITION OF THE UNITED KINGDOM UNDER A SCHEME OF PREFERENTIAL TARIFFS WITH INDIA

WE now come to a discussion of the effect upon British trade with India of a system of preferential tariffs within the Empire. There is one preliminary question which needs to be discussed. The advocates of protection and preference have continually insisted that the United Kingdom is not maintaining its position in the Indian markets. The Tariff Commission has published its statistics on the subject, and comes to the conclusion that our share of Indian trade shows a "continuous decline."[1] Since these may be regarded as the most authoritative figures by which this view can be supported, we

[1] Memo. 38 of the Tariff Commission, entitled "The Trade Relations of India with the United Kingdom, British Possessions, and Foreign Countries," Part I.

shall examine them. The following are the statistics of the import trade of India for 1906—7.[1]

Value of total imports of private merchandise from all countries into British India	£72,205,000
Value of total imports of private merchandise from United Kingdom into British India	£48,199,000

The United Kingdom therefore holds 67 per cent. of the import trade of India. This appears, at first sight, to be a highly satisfactory position. It is, however, regarded by the advocates of a preferential system as furnishing causes for grave alarm. The reason for this opinion is that they compare it with our position a generation ago. The Tariff Commission, for example, points out that in 1885 the statistics were as follows:—

Value of total imports of private merchandise from all countries into British India	£41,557,000[2]

[1] "Statistical Abstract for British India for 1908," p. 147.

[2] Memo. 38 of Tariff Commission, p. 4.

Value of total imports of private merchandise from United Kingdom into British India £33,414,000

In 1885, therefore, the United Kingdom held 80 per cent. of the import trade of India compared with 67 per cent. in 1906—7. This is the "continuous decline" which the Tariff Commission has revealed, while another authority invites us to view these figures with "horror and alarm."[1] Before accepting this invitation, let us compare our position with that of our more serious competitors. The following table makes this clear :—

IMPORTS OF PRIVATE MERCHANDISE INTO BRITISH INDIA FROM PRINCIPAL COUNTRIES.

	1805—6.	1906—7.	Increase.
	£	£	£
United Kingdom .	33,414,000	48,199,000	14,785,000
Germany . . .	96,000	3,861,000	3,765,000
Belgium . . .	412,000	2,904,000	2,492,000
Austria-Hungary .	362,000	2,046,000	1,684,000
United States . .	660,000	1,698,000	1,030,000
Japan	19,000	1,073,000	1,054,000
All foreign countries	3,865,000	18,448,000	14,583,000[2]

[1] "India and Imperial Preference," by Sir Roper Lethbridge, p. 21.

[2] Memo. 38 of Tariff Commission, p. 4.

The increase of our imports, therefore, has been four times as great as that of any other nation, and slightly greater than that of all the other nations of the world taken together. These are figures on which we might well look with pride. Yet they are the same as those used by the Tariff Commission to prove the steady decrease of our trade. The explanation is that the statistics of the Tariff Commission are based upon a false premise. It is assumed that British imports, starting from a base of £33,000,000, ought to increase in the same proportion as those of nations which started from a base of a few thousand pounds. If they fail to do this they are held to exhibit a "continuous decline." This is an example of the error well known to statisticians of using percentages without reference to amounts. "In the beginning of things percentages may be large, as we all know, but the real growth may be largest where the percentage is least, in consequence of the greater amount at which the percentage is calcu-

lated."[1] This warning against a very obvious mistake is continually neglected in our tariff discussions, and the figures that we are criticising furnish an unusually glaring example of the error.

We can now proceed to our main task and estimate the effect of preferences with India upon British trade. For this purpose we shall examine first Great Britain's possibilities of gain, next her possibilities of loss, so that we shall then be in a position to conclude which of the two appear the greater. The statistics of Indian imports for 1906—7 were as follows:—

Total imports of private merchandise into British India, £72,205,000.

Imports from United Kingdom, £48,199,000.

Imports from British colonies, £5,558,000.

Imports from foreign countries, £18,448,000.[2]

[1] Giffen, "Economic Studies and Enquiries," Vol. I., p. 286.

[2] "Statistical Abstract for British India for 1908," p. 147.

The sum of £18,448,000 due to imports from foreign countries represents all the trade which might be diverted to the United Kingdom by a preference in her favour. A large proportion, however, of these imports are of such a nature that even with a preference the United Kingdom could not take the place of the existing source of supply. The following come within this category:—

	Value of Imports from outside British Empire.
Dyeing and tanning materials ...	£631,000
Fruits and vegetables	60,000
Grain and pulse	188,000
Gums and resin	139,000
Hides and skins, pressed and tanned	178,000
Horses	68,000
Oil	1,529,000
Raw silk	323,000
Spices	16,000
Sugar...	4,151,000
Tea	89,000
Wood and manufactures of ...	574,000
Raw wool	58,000
	£8,004,000[1]

[1] These figures are calculated from those given in the "Statistical Abstract for British India for 1906—7," pp. 149 and 167—180.

The value, therefore, of the imports of which the supply from the United Kingdom can be effective is reduced to £10,444,000. But what proportion of these imports would be captured by British merchants in consequence of the preference? To this question no definite answer is possible, but the general result is clear. As foreign countries hold less than a quarter of the import trade, and as even of this proportion 43 per cent. consists of commodities in which the United Kingdom cannot effectively compete, the gain from a preference cannot be very substantial. The Government of India has come to the same conclusion. In the official statement of their views they lay down their opinion that "a preference of one-fourth calculated on a very low rate of duty would be of very little material advantage to British manufacturers," and they go on to point out that this represents as much as India can offer.[1]

[1] "Views of the Government of India on the Question of Preferential Tariffs," p. 8.

The next step in our enquiry is to estimate what the United Kingdom would lose in payment for the preference in India. The British position is difficult, for the bulk of the commodities for which India would justly demand a reciprocal preference are exactly of the kind to which we cannot afford to offer anything appreciable. The following are our chief imports from India :—

IMPORTS INTO GREAT BRITAIN FROM INDIA FOR 1906—7.

Raw jute	£7,700,000
Tea	5,000,000
Wheat	4,400,000
Hides, raw, pressed and tanned...	3,200,000
Oil seeds	2,200,000
Raw wool	1,500,000
Jute manufactures	1,200,000
Raw cotton	860,000
Rice...	840,000
Lac...	600,000

These ten articles represent 90 per cent. of the total value of British imports from

[1] "Statistical Abstract for British India for 1907—8," p. 168.

India. They can be divided into three classes:—

(1) Articles in which a preference is a practical impossibility—

Raw jute.

Lac.

Tea.

Jute manufactures.

India possesses a practical monopoly of raw jute and lac. There are no competitors to defend her against, and a preference is therefore impossible.

The position of her tea industry is somewhat similar. It has been pointed out that Chinese tea has been almost entirely driven out of the British market. Of the tea imported into the United Kingdom in 1907,

59 per cent. came from India.

31 per cent. came from Ceylon.

3 per cent. came from China.

7 per cent. came from other countries.[1]

Thus India's only serious competitor is

[1] "Annual Statement of the Trade of the United Kingdom," Vol. I., p. 314.

Ceylon, which would, of course, be included equally with her in any preferential scheme. Again, therefore, India has practically nothing to gain.

Almost the same reasoning applies to her jute manufactures. Eighty-nine per cent. of our imports of jute manufactures comes from India.[1] Her only effective rival, therefore, is Dundee, but as, of course, no preference will give her an advantage over British goods again, we have nothing substantial to offer her.

The four commodities that we have considered represent 46 per cent. of the value of British imports from India. If the United Kingdom is to offer any substantial preference it must be in the remaining imports. These, however, consist either of raw materials essential to British industries or of articles of food:—

(2) Hides.
Oil seeds.

[1] "Annual Statement of Trade of United Kingdom for 1909," Vol. I., p. 194.

Raw wool.
Raw cotton.

Each of these is a necessity to our manufactures of which an appreciable rise in price would not be tolerated. This, indeed, is a conclusion inherent in the reasoning of the Tariff Commission and of other advocates of preference. They have continually insisted that India has nothing to fear from the retaliation of foreign nations, for her exports to them consist of raw materials of which they cannot afford to raise the price.[1] We accept this reasoning, as will be seen in the next chapter; but it applies to the United Kingdom with no less force than to foreign countries. The articles are as essential to our industries as to those of our competitors, and a rise in the price would be equally injurious. India's only remaining exports of importance are—

(3) Wheat.
Rice.

They, however, are articles of food of

[1] Tariff Commission, Memo. 30, p. 17.

which no substantial rise in price will be permitted in Great Britain. Besides, in the case of wheat such small preference as is proposed is offered equally to Canada and other colonies.

The position of Great Britain is, therefore, that she cannot offer any fair reciprocal advantage to India without a substantial rise in the price either of raw materials, on which some of her important industries depend, or of food stuffs.[1] This is the first item of her payment for a preference in India. If she proposes honestly to offer a fair return she must face a serious loss in this direction. This is not a very hopeful situation, but we come now to further consequences of the utmost gravity which in all discussions up to the present have been relegated to the background.

India, it has been explained, is intensely protectionist. The arguments in favour of

[1] There are a few other minor imports on which it has been argued that we might offer a preference. These are considered in the next chapter.

protection in India are, indeed, much stronger than in the United Kingdom. In any scheme of preference the first question which will confront Great Britain is whether India is to be allowed to follow the example of the self-governing colonies. Is she to be permitted to erect a protective tariff against British goods? Permission to do this has been refused up to the present, but we must examine the reasons given for this action. Great Britain has always maintained, as her honour demanded, that she would never subordinate the good of India to the selfish interests of British manufacturers. She has been able to force free trade upon India because she has argued, with complete consistency, that she believed that it was for India's good and that she applied the same principles to herself. Our position has been clearly defined during the course of the protracted negotiations over the cotton duties. When the cotton industry began to assume large proportions Great Britain insisted that it should not grow up under a protective tariff.

After a lengthy discussion the principles on which we were acting were laid down in 1876 in a despatch from Lord Salisbury, the Secretary of State for India. He did not deny that the interests of British manufacturers were concerned, but he insisted that this fact would not have determined the decision of it if it had not been that free trade was essential to India herself. He argued that the duties would encourage the cotton industry to grow up under unhealthy conditions instead of in the bracing atmosphere of free trade, and would thus expose it to future injury. "Whether," he concluded, "the question be regarded as it affects the consumer, the producer, or the revenue, I am of opinion that the interests of India imperatively require the removal of a tax which is at once wrong in principle, injurious in its practical effect, and self-destructive in its operation."

In the same spirit the House of Commons based their support of this decision on the general principle that free trade was as applicable, in their opinion, to India as to Great Britain.

"The duties now levied upon cotton manufactures imported into India, being protective in their nature, are contrary to sound commercial policy, and ought to be repealed without delay so soon as the financial condition of India will permit."

The duties were practically abolished in 1879. Although the Viceroy, Lord Lytton, had to act in opposition to the majority of his Council, he was supported by his finance minister, Sir John Strachey. It is instructive to read Sir John Strachey's repudiation of the charge that the interests of India were being sacrificed to those of Great Britain:—

"Popular opinion in India had always, in regard to questions of fiscal reform, been obstructive and ignorant; and the fact that the abolition of customs duties would be favourable to English manufactures was enough, in the belief of many, to prove that the party purpose of obtaining political support in Lancashire, and not any care for the interests of India, was the real motive of the Government. This foolish calumny deserved no notice nor reply. The opposition to the reform of the cotton duties satisfied Lord Lytton that he must carry out the measure himself or acquiesce in nothing being done at all. He believed that the interest of India required it, and he was not to be deterred by the imputation of base motives."[1]

It is not necessary to quote the declarations which have since been made by Government, or the resolutions passed by the House of Commons. Throughout them we have maintained, as we were in honour bound to do, that we should not force India to adopt free trade if we did not believe that we were acting for her good. This attitude was perfectly justifiable as long as Great Britain herself upheld free trade. But what will her position be if she herself abandons it? British statesmen will be faced by two alternatives. It is possible for them to assert unashamedly that India is merely a

[1] "India," by John Strachey, p. 178.

"plantation" whose good must be sacrificed to the interests of British capital. They can acknowledge that their arguments and pledges in the past were mere hypocrisy which, having served their purpose, can now be abandoned. This alternative is, of course, inconceivable. The only other is to grant India her fiscal freedom and to allow her to erect a protective tariff.

There can no longer be any doubt whether the balance lies on the side of loss or gain. The very fact that Great Britain holds such a predominant position in the Indian market now turns against her. As only one-fourth of the imports of India comes from foreign nations, an Indian tariff must from the nature of the conditions strike chiefly at British goods. Taking the imports from each country as a rough measure of its loss, the damage inflicted upon Great Britain will be more than twelve times as great as upon any other nation, and from twice to three times as great as upon all other nations put together. In all proposals for the reversal of our fiscal system India has been kept in the background, and attention has been concentrated upon the markets in the self-governing colonies. Yet the Indian market for our goods is not much smaller than that of all the self-governing colonies taken together.[1]

The effect of tariff reform upon our trade with India would therefore be one of the governing factors which would determine the ultimate result of the scheme. There is no doubt that it would strike a heavy blow at our trade in the best market which the world now offers to us.[2]

[1] In 1907 our exports to all the self-governing colonies taken together were worth £64,069,696, while our exports to India were worth £52,103,796.—"Statistical Abstract for United Kingdom for 1909," p. 153.

Our exports to India are greater than to any other country in the world.

CHAPTER VII

THE POSITION OF INDIA UNDER A SCHEME OF PREFERENTIAL TARIFFS

Is India likely to obtain any advantage from preferences within the United Kingdom? Most of the work needed to answer this question has been done in the last chapter. We have seen that, as regards the ten chief exports from India to the United Kingdom, representing 90 per cent. of the total, no preference is possible unless we are willing to raise the price of raw materials essential to our industries or of food stuffs. From the nature of our conditions, therefore, we have nothing substantial to offer. What our proposals would actually be can only be conjectured until a definite tariff is laid before us. It would probably be found that Great Britain had no intention of imposing any handicap upon her industries by raising the prices of materials necessary to them. Our offer would thus reduce itself to a preference on wheat and rice to be shared with the remainder of the Empire.

This is the conclusion so far as India's important exports to us are concerned. As a result, however, of the poverty of any possible offer from us on their account, much stress has been laid upon the advantages that we could give to certain other Indian exports. These consist of sugar, indigo, tobacco, and coffee.[1] All of them occupy minor positions in our list of imports from India, but we will examine their prospects of gain.

We have already pointed out more than once that the stationary condition of the sugar industry is due to causes which tariffs will not cure. The imports into the United Kingdom are rapidly decreasing. Their

[1] See Sir Edward Law's memorandum on "Views of the Government of India on the Question of Preferential Tariffs."

value in 1897—8 was £126,000, but by 1906—7 it had sunk to £37,000. A preference would need to have very remarkable effects to counteract the deep-seated causes of this decline. The results which we have seen to follow from the direct protection given by the countervailing duties have not been of a character which leads us to expect much from the indirect protection of a preference in the United Kingdom.[1]

The expectations formed of the effect of preferences upon the indigo industry appear extravagant. Here we have an example of the conflict between the older methods of production and the wonderful achievements of modern science. There can be little doubt of its eventual result. The area under indigo in India has, during the last nine years, shrunk to one-third of its former size. The exports to the United Kingdom have steadily diminished during the same period, and their value now is only one-quarter of what it was nine years

[1] See pp. 40—43.

ago.[1] A preference may have some little effect in making inevitable decline slightly less rapid, but Sir Edward Law's opinion that as the result of it "the difficulties of our indigo planters would disappear as by magic," is clearly extravagant.

Such exaggerated claims have not been put forward on behalf of the two remaining commodities—coffee and tobacco. The area under coffee in India is steadily declining, while the exports to the United Kingdom exhibit great fluctuations, with a tendency to diminish.[2] The trade has been severely damaged by the competition of cheap Brazilian coffee, and a preference might be of some assistance to it. It would, besides, be comparatively easy to give, as it would not involve the imposition of any fresh duties, but merely the remission or lowering of the existing duty on the Indian import.

[1] The value has decreased from £435,000 in 1897—8 to £110,000 in 1906.—"Statistical Abstract for British India for 1908," p. 168.

[2] "Statistical Abstract for British India for 1908," p. 168.

Apart from any claim for preference, the Indian tobacco industry has a legitimate grievance. The British duty is charged at a certain rate per pound instead of *ad valorem*. As the Indian tobacco is of low value, the effect is to compel it to pay a higher *ad valorem* duty than its competitors. If this grievance were removed, and at the same time a preference were given to it, the Indian industry ought certainly to be stimulated to some extent. It is, however, impossible at present to judge whether the effect would be of any great importance, as the exports to the United Kingdom are quite insignificant. Their total value in 1906—7, including that of both manufactured and unmanufactured tobacco, amounted to only a little over £16,000.[1]

Whatever may be the precise result of preference upon these four minor exports, the prospects which the policy offers to India must be judged mainly by its effects upon

[1] "Statistics of the Sea-borne Trade and Navigation of British India," Vol. I., pp. 441, 442.

the staple exports, which are of real significance. We therefore return to the fact that, so far as they are concerned, the United Kingdom is not in a position to make an offer worth serious consideration. Our general conclusion is that India has little either to lose or gain by being included in a preferential scheme with the United Kingdom.

We have not yet examined the position of the colonies and dependencies, because they would only hold a very minor place in any scheme of preferences with India. The self-governing colonies would probably have no place at all, as their trade with India is too small. In 1902 the value of India's imports from Canada was less than £2,000, from New Zealand less than £6,000, from Cape Colony less than £2,000, and from Natal less than £4,000.[1] No preference is possible on such figures as these, and we are left with Australia, whose imports were

[1] "Statistical Abstract for British India for 1908," pp. 173, 174, 180.

worth £467,000, as the one self-governing colony whose trade with India is not negligible. The only large item in this £467,000 is the import of horses, which represents £231,000. Australia, however, already holds 85 per cent. of the sea-borne trade in horses, so that there is little room for preference here.[1]

Turning to the dependencies, the imports from most of them into India are too insignificant to furnish a basis for preference. With four of them, however—British East Africa, Ceylon, the Straits Settlements and Mauritius—the trade assumes proportions large enough to demand consideration.

The imports from British East Africa in 1906 were worth £141,000. Of this sum £105,000 was due to spices, which are the only imports of sufficient value to make any preference effective. The only serious competitors, however, are Ceylon and the Straits Settlements. The value of their combined

[1] "Statistical Abstract for British India for 1907," p. 180.

imports of spices into India amounts to £835,000, while only £16,000 worth comes from countries outside the Empire. As any preference would include Ceylon and the Straits Settlements, it is evident that British East Africa has practically nothing to gain.[1]

Ceylon, for the same reason, has nothing to expect from a preference for her exports of spices to India. Her remaining export of importance is cocoanut oil. India receives this to the value of £117,000, and at the same time buys from foreign countries vegetable oils worth £110,000. A duty on the latter, therefore, might be of some slight advantage to Ceylon.[2]

Putting out of account, for reasons already given, the spices of the Straits Settlements, we are left with mineral oil as their only other export to India of sufficient importance

[1] "Statistical Abstract for British India for 1908," pp. 149, 173, 177, 179.

[2] "Statistical Abstract for British India for 1908," pp. 149, 176.

to make preference worth considering. Since, however, India's imports of this commodity from the Straits Settlements are worth £112,000, while the value of her imports from foreign countries amounts to £1,400,000, it will be seen that preference would necessitate the dislocation of a large foreign trade for the sake of a comparatively small trade from the Straits Settlements.[1] If preference only were involved it is doubtful whether such a dislocation would be justified. But it has already been explained that a protective duty on mineral oil is not improbable. If this were imposed it would be easy to introduce into it a preference for the oil from the Straits Settlements.

The case of Mauritius is the simplest of the group. India imports sugar to the value of £1,400,000 from Mauritius, as compared with a value of £4,150,000 from foreign

[1] "Statistical Abstract for British India for 1908,' pp. 149, 179.

countries.[1] There is thus a strong basis for preference, while the precedent for it has already been established by the countervailing duties. If, therefore, the Indian sugar planters succeed in enforcing their demand for protection, a preference for Mauritius would be a natural accompaniment. The Straits Settlements, Mauritius, and perhaps Ceylon, thus emerge as the dependencies which would reap an advantage from a preference.

The next question which arises is, whether they can offer any reciprocal benefit to India. They all draw large supplies of rice from India for their plantation coolies. But she already has a practical monopoly in the supply of this article in Ceylon and Mauritius. We are therefore left with the Straits Settlements as the only colony in which Indian trade might be assisted by a preference.

The introduction of the colonies into our discussion of the subject has not caused us

[1] "Statistical Abstract for British India for 1908,' pp. 149, 173, 178.

to move away from the conclusion already reached, that India has equally little either to lose or gain from a scheme of preferential tariffs within the Empire. The results for Great Britain can be more definitely stated. British trade will suffer a staggering blow, for we shall be confronted by a protective tariff in the only great free market which we now enjoy.

[1] The proper action for Indian administrators and publicists to take in view of the conclusions of this chapter is discussed in the Preface.

INDEX

BRADBURY, AGNEW, & CO. LD., PRINTERS, LONDON AND TONBRIDGE.